SECRETS OF MENTALLY STRONG PEOPLE

HOW TO BUILD RESILIENCE AND BE DONE WITH MENTAL BAD HABITS

SMITH JONES

Copyright © 2022 SMITH JONES

All rights reserved

The characters and events portrayed in this book are fictitious. Any similarity to real persons, living or dead, is coincidental and not intended by the author.

No part of this book may be reproduced, or stored in a retrieval system, or transmitted in any form or by any means, electronic, mechanical, photocopying, recording, or otherwise, without express written permission of the publisher.

ISBN: 9798419575141

*This book is dedicated to those who are
ready to advance in the self performance
better than they used to be and are ready
to take up a journey into this.*

CONTENTS

Title Page

Copyright

Dedication

INTRODUCTION	1
3 Warning Signs That You Lack the Mental Strength To Lead	6
SECRETS OF MENTALLY STRONG INDIVIDUALS.	12
SIGNS OF A MENTALLY STRONG PERSON	16
WHY MENTALLY STRONG PEOPLE USUALLY SUCCEED IN ANY SITUATION	39
THE 4 C'S OF MENTAL TOUGHNESS:	44
STEP BY STEP INSTRUCTIONS TO BUILD RESILIENCE IN ADULTS	47
10 TIPS TO BUILD RESILIENCE IN TEENS AND YOUNG ADULTS	48
HOW TO INCREASE MENTAL STRENGTH IN STUDENTS	54

ALTERNATE WAYS OF BUILDING AND 58
FURTHER DEVELOPING FLEXIBILITY

FURTHER SYSTEMS 61

INTRODUCTION

Many individuals might want to have the option to manage all of the high points and low points life tosses them with a tranquil strength and elegance. Be that as it may, this isn't dependably a simple errand. Turning out to be intellectually solid isn't something that you can simply choose to do, and it for the most part doesn't occur out of the blue.

Being intellectually and sincerely compelling implies that you can act ordinarily regardless of how much pressure is introduced. As such, you can continue ahead regardless occurs.

Furthermore, it's significantly harder than it sounds.

• Whenever you're mentally strong, you can inspire yourself. You needn't bother with others to do it for you. You can get up and make a beeline for the exercise center with no external inspiration. You get up and clean yourself off after a fall with no consolation from others. You get it done. Enough said.

• Whenever you're mentally strong, you go up against yourself rather than your friends. You know what you did yesterday, and you need to improve tomorrow. This assists you with continuously defining reasonable objectives.

- At the point when you're mentally strong, others notice. It rouses them and permits you to be the pioneer. You probably won't see that you play to become a part model to other people. It's exactly who you are currently.

- Whenever you're mentally strong, you look at reality without flinching unafraid. You face the difficult things in life as opposed to fleeing from the hard stuff.

- Mental Strength is the limit of a person to manage stressors, tensions, and difficulties and perform surprisingly well, regardless of the conditions wherein they get themselves

- Developing mental strength is central to carrying on with your best life. Similarly, as we go to the gym and lift loads to fabricate our actual muscles, we should likewise foster our psychological wellness using mental instruments and procedures.

- Ideal emotional wellness assists us with carrying on with a daily existence that we love, have significant social associations, and have positive confidence. It additionally supports our capacity to face challenges, attempt new things, and adapt to any tough spots that life might toss at us.

- Mental strength includes growing everyday

propensities that form mental muscle. It likewise includes surrendering negative quirks that keep you down.

• To be intellectually solid, we should develop our psychological fortitude! Mental strength is something created after some time by people who decide to focus on self-improvement. Similar to seeing actual additions from working out and eating better, we should foster sound mental propensities, such as rehearsing appreciation, to encounter emotional wellness gains.

• In like manner, to see actual increases we should likewise surrender unfortunate things to do, like eating low-quality food, and for mental additions, surrender undesirable propensities, for example, feeling frustrated about oneself.

• We are on the whole ready to turn out to be intellectually more grounded, the key is to continue rehearsing and practicing your psychological muscles - similarly as you would if you were attempting to develop actual fortitude!

• Mentally strong individual is a one who oversees in his/all her sentiments, possibly it ought to be controlled or to communicate.

• Mental strongness implies that nobody could obliterate your inner harmony.

• As indicated by my rationale, each individual has some attitude about everything, about society, about future, about guardians, about transporter, about kinship, connections, and so on...

- Furthermore changes are the law of nature so the attitude changes as per time, age, and experience. Through this change, the person who could deal with the essential guideline of his/her personality is supposed to be a mentally strong individual.

- As a model, when we go for higher examinations to some school or inn, there are such countless things expected to be changed. Very much like you want not to respond if somebody is attempting liquor since they think that it's the age to take a stab at everything. The one needs to get that assuming difficult liquor is terrible for an understudy life, as indicated by his/her past mentality then they have not to attempt it in any situation.

- It's not the extraordinary arrangement assuming you would be perceived as a humble community kid/young lady, yet drinking liquor or effectively demonstrating that you are progressed is thoroughly off-base.

- I'm not saying that don't change your laid out set of attitude however transform it positively and change it when it needs not for the hotshot.

- The person who apologizes for his/her responsibility is likewise from one of the significant images to be a mentally strong individual, even an individual ought to have a feck to concur what he/she did.

- Mental toughness is a perspective that assuming you realize that you are correct, you can go intensive the contrary stream regardless the general public matters. However, going through this you should initially identify that you are correct.

- To be mentally strong means to adjust well notwithstanding difficulty, injury, misfortune, dangers, or critical wellsprings of stress. An intellectually solid individual has great adapting abilities and solid strength.

- A mentally strong individual won't allow dread to stop him/her from pushing ahead. Mentally strong individuals have solid personalities, they know who they are what can be done. They comprehend the conduct of others and figure out how to excuse and give up. They know how to assume liability for their activities and how to trust in themselves.

3 WARNING SIGNS THAT YOU LACK THE MENTAL STRENGTH TO LEAD

Leadership isn't something you pronounce; it's something you demonstrate. Do you have the psychological solidarity to lead? Do you have the mental strength to make the life, vocation, and encounters you need?

Here is reality. You have this life-this one life-to investigate what intrigues you and construct a fruitful profession. You have a voice-and an inward and external voice-that you can use to all the more likely express and impart your thoughts and requirements. You have options a few reality and professional decisions that you should make to encounter a new thing or unique. You have a mind, your brain which you should have, and control to turn out to be more focused. Furthermore, whether or not you know it, you have the power-genuine ability to direct and lead your way.

Yet, it's solely after you choose to lead yourself first-your life, your voice, your decisions, and your mind that you can employ your power so that you effectively make the progressions you look for. Honestly, leadership is hard. Discipline is hard, and controlling your brain is hard, however, mentally strong individuals effectively arrange and adjust every one of the three to make and support progress.

Do you have the mental strength to lead yourself as well as other people? The following are three unmistakable practices that sound a caution proposing that you could not.

1. You apologize for your aspiration and your prosperity.

Intellectually solid pioneers aren't hesitant to reach higher, and they aren't humiliated by or embarrassed about their prosperity. With more noteworthy degrees of achievement come more prominent degrees of analysis. Whenever you have the psychological solidarity to lead, you exhibit the psychological guts to overlook the critics.

Assuming that you wind up saying 'sorry' for thinking beyond practical boundaries and attempting to achieve your objectives, stop it. If you are saying 'sorry' for your responsibility, stop it. If you apologize for your capability, stop it. If you wind up saying 'sorry' for your decisions, stop it. Some will attempt to cause you to feel regretful for your prosperity. They could attempt to because you to feel like open doors are some way or another just given to you to the prohibition of most others, particularly them.

Some might attempt to cause you to feel regretful for being focused to the point of making progress.

Try not to be. Except if you misunderstand done somebody or hold others down to get where you are, the reason could you apologize? Invest in some opportunity to help other people excel and add to their prosperity. Hoist another's expected when and where you can. There is a few genuine worth and euphoria in doing that. Be that as it may, don't go around saying 'sorry' for your certainty or for accomplishing the difficult work to accomplish what you need. What's more, don't endure others asking you to.

Suppose you've fizzled at certain things throughout everyday life. Alright, we all have. Suppose you've disheartened certain individuals on your excursion. OK, we all have. Suppose you've settled on a few terrible choices and battled intellectually and inwardly. Alright, we all have. Suppose you've been dismissed; surely, we all have. Suppose you once in a while battle with certainty and weakness. Alright, we all do. The point here is that it's not unexpected ordinary and approve to be human. Furthermore being you implies that you're somewhat flawed. You commit errors, you mess up, you fall and you even come up short. It implies that you don't constantly make the best choice and that you haven't lived up all the time to your own beliefs and potential.

Surely, if you have a few things to set things straight for, do that. Set forth the energy to right your wrongs any place you can. Set forth the energy to reconstruct and sustain connections that make a difference to you. Set forth the energy to offer to set things right. However, if in the wake of doing all of this, you see that individuals around you make you feel not exactly or they some way or another keep you from embracing your power, you need to return to a stage to deal with you. Assuming you observe that in the wake of cooperating with specific individuals your frailties are increased and your certainty is brought down, you should show the mental strength to continue.

2. You contrast your life and profession with others.

Mentally strong individuals are too bustling watering their grass to stress over how green-or, not another's a grass is. Whenever you have the psychological solidarity to lead, you praise the achievement and accomplishments of others, yet you don't sit around idly or energy with comparison. It's a pointless exercise and a worthless method for estimating your life, your disappointments, your achievements, or your victories.

At the point when you contrast yourself with others' results without knowing the sources of info and penances they needed to place in or make to arrive, you are ill-fated to encounter dissatisfaction, floundering, jealousy, or something more regrettable. At the point when you measure your life or profession against others without enthusiasm for the scandalous little secrets and sacrifices they made to get where they are, you lose.

Individuals show what they need us to see. Individuals praise their victories rather than their disappointments. They share the large successes, not the staggering misfortunes. They introduce themselves to the world after they've gotten back up rather than while they were tumbling down. Individuals will more often than not share pictures and accounts of euphoria and grins instead of torment and tears. Individuals will quite often share what they get acknowledged to rather than what they got dismissed from.

Mentally strong leaders know not to at any point take part in this game. Rather than estimating your satisfaction and accomplishment against others, I suggest you measure yourself against yourself. Measure your accomplishment of today against yesterday, how focused you are this month rather than last month, and your development this year instead of last. Set your bar. Mentally strong individuals measure their lives and vocations against their norms, and they measure their practices and decisions against their own genuine goals.

Demonstrate mental strength.

Mentally strong leaders track down the strength to cherish themselves; they track down the solidarity to give up. They track down the solidarity to foster new emotionally supportive networks of individuals who can all the more likely like their gifts and commend their brightness.

Mentally strong leaders center around what they can handle. They set their principles for progress. And keeping in mind that they in all actuality do take ownership of their errors and apologize for bad behavior, mentally strong leaders don't go around saying 'sorry' for what their identity is. All things being equal, intellectually solid pioneers own their ability to lead, and they own their ability to impact positive change. Do you have the mental strength to do this? Assuming this is the case, it's an indication that you have the mental strength to lead.

SECRETS OF MENTALLY STRONG INDIVIDUALS.

Here are significant and consistent things mentally strong individuals do.

Remembering their good fortune, rather than their weight, assists mentally strong individuals with keeping life in a legitimate viewpoint. Their decision to be thankful radiates through in their disposition and conduct.

Mentally strong individuals don't give pessimistic individuals control over them. They will not fault anybody for keeping them down or hauling them down.

Mentally strong individuals view difficulty as a valuable chance to develop further. With each obstacle they survive, they gain trust in their capacity to turn out to be better.

Mentally strong individuals stay useful and successful by zeroing in on the things they have command over. Instead of squandering energy stressing over whether the tempest will come, they put their endeavors into planning for it all that can be expected.

Making sound enthusiastic and actual limits gives

mentally resilient individuals the room they need to develop. In any event, when they might dishearten others, they're willing to say no.

Mentally strong individuals offset their feelings with rationale so they can work out each hazard they face. They're willing to venture outside their usual range of familiarity and look for open doors that will assist them with arriving at their objectives.

Mentally strong individuals ponder the past so they can gain from it, yet they don't harp on it. They will not carry on with an existence of disappointment and they let go of hard feelings.

Instead of thumping themselves for their errors, intellectually resilient individuals center around gaining from them. They acknowledge full liability regarding their conduct and decide to push ahead in a useful way.

As opposed to disliking others' favorable luck, mentally strong individuals go ahead and share in their satisfaction. They perceive that others' accomplishments don't lessen their own.

Disappointment is regularly essential for any lengthy excursion toward progress. Intellectually resilient individuals acknowledge that and they decide to involve every disappointment as a chance to become more astute.

Intellectually tough individuals invest in some opportunity to be separated from everyone else with their contemplations. Regardless of whether they write in a diary, practice contemplation, or sit quietly and reflect, they realize a little isolation is essential to their prosperity.

Mentally strong individuals set out open doors for themselves. They don't sit around trusting that the world will give them the thought process they're owed. They realize that the best things in life merit hanging tight. They practice tolerance and steadiness as they make progress toward their objectives. They won't permit self-restricting convictions to confine their true capacity. They comprehend their psyches can be their best resource or their most terrible adversary.

Rather than griping about things they can't change or reiterating something that happened yesterday, mentally strong individuals dedicate their energy to useful assignments. They don't squander restricted assets, similar to time and energy, on things that aren't useful.

Mentally strong individuals converse with themselves like a confided-in mentor. They will not accept pessimistic forecasts however they likewise don't permit themselves to become pompous. They aren't reluctant to bear a little aggravation. Regardless of whether they continue to run when their legs are drained or they oppose moment delight, they practice self-restraint in any event, when it's awkward.

Mentally strong individuals keep their needs following their convictions. They're adequately fearless to live as per their qualities, in any event, when it's not the well-known decision.

SIGNS OF A MENTALLY STRONG PERSON

It's fine and good to know a rundown of characteristics shared by resilient individuals, yet how would you perceive those characteristics in yourself or others?

Search for the accompanying practices as indications of becoming stronger.

1. You're Slow to Anger.

You don't get unsettled without any problem. You've learned not to make others' words and moves actually or to make suppositions about others' aims toward you. You by and large figure out how to try to avoid panicking in any event, when the vast majority think that it is troublesome.

Outrage is an ordinary inclination and can be a positive feeling when it assists you with taking care of problems or issues, regardless of whether that is working or at home.

Nonetheless, outrage can become dangerous assuming that it prompts animosity, eruptions, or even actual squabbles.

Outrage control is significant for assisting you with abstaining from saying or accomplishing something you might lament. Before outrage raises, you can involve explicit procedures for controlling displeasure.

The following are 25 different ways you can handle your anger:

1. Count down

Count down (or up) to 10. If you're truly distraught, begin at 100. In the time it takes you to count, your pulse will slow, and your resentment will probably die down.

2. Take a load off

Your breathing becomes shallower and speeds up as you become angry. Turn around that pattern (and your resentment) by taking sluggish, full breaths from your nose and breathing out of your mouth for a very long time.

3. Go stroll around

Practice Believed Source can assist with quieting your nerves and decreasing outrage. Take a walk, ride your bicycle, or hit a couple of golf balls. Whatever gets your limbs pumping is great for your psyche and body.

4. Loosen up your muscles

Moderate muscle unwinding approaches you to tense and gradually loosen up different muscle bunches in your body, each in turn. As you tense and deliver, take slow, intentional breaths.

5. Repeat a mantra

Track down a word or expression that helps you quiet down and pull together. Repeat that word and again to yourself when you're disturbed. "Unwind," "Relax, and "You'll be alright" are generally genuine models.

6. Stretch

Neck rolls and shoulder rolls are genuine instances of nonstrenuous yoga-like developments that can assist you with controlling your body and outfitting your feelings. No extravagant gear is required.

7. Mentally escape

Slip into a tranquil room, shut your eyes, and work on picturing yourself in a loosening up scene. Zero in on subtleties in the fanciful scene: What tone is the water? How tall are the mountains? What do the peeping birds sound like? This training can assist you with tracking down quiet amid outrage.

8. Play a few tunes

Allow the music to divert you from your sentiments. Put in earbuds or get out to your vehicle. Wrench up your beloved music and murmur, bop, or sashay your outrage away.

9. Quiet down

At the point when you're steamed, you might be enticed to allow the furious words to fly, yet you're bound to cause more damage than great. Imagine your lips are stuck closed, very much as you did as a child. This second without talking will allow you to gather your contemplations.

10. Take a break

Offer yourself a reprieve. Sit away from others. In this tranquil time, you can deal with occasions and return your feelings to unbiased. You might even figure out this opportunity away from others is so useful you need to plan it into your everyday schedule.

11. Make a move

Bridle your anger energy. Sign an appeal. Compose a note to an authority. Help another person. Empty your energy and feelings into something sound and useful.

12. Write in your diary

What you can't say, maybe you can compose. Write down the thing you're feeling and how you need to react. Handling it through the composed word can help you quiet down and rethink the occasions paving the way to your sentiments.

13. Track down the quickest arrangement

Yet again you may be furious that your kid has left their room a wreck before going to visit a companion. Close the entryway. You can briefly end your indignation by putting it out of your view. Search for comparative goals in any circumstances.

14. Practice your reaction

Forestall an explosion by practicing what you will say or how you will move toward the issue later on. This practice period allows you to pretend a few potential arrangements, as well.

15. Picture a stop sign

The general image to stop can assist you with quieting down when you're irate. It's a speedy method for assisting you with imagining the need to end yourself, your activities, and leave the occasion.

16. Change your daily practice

If your sluggish drive to work drives you mad before you've even had espresso, track down another course. Consider choices that might take longer however leave you less furious eventually.

17. Converse with a companion

Try not to stew in the occasions that drove you mad. Assist yourself with handling what occurred by chatting with a trusted, steady companion who might potentially give another viewpoint.

18. Chuckle

Nothing overturns a terrible mindset like a decent one. Diffuse your resentment by searching for ways of chuckling, regardless of whether that is playing with your children, watching stand-up, or looking over images.

19. Practice appreciation

Pause for a minute to zero into what's right side when all that feels wrong. Acknowledging the number of beneficial things you have in your life can assist you with killing outrage and pivoting what is happening.

20. Set a clock

The main thing that strikes a chord when you're irate likely isn't what you should say. Give yourself a set time before you react. This time will assist you with being quieter and more succinct.

21. Compose a letter

Compose a letter or email to the individual that drove you mad. Then, at that point, erase it. Regularly, communicating your feelings in some structure is all you need, regardless of whether it's in something that won't ever be seen.

22. Envision excusing them

Tracking down the fortitude to excuse somebody who has violated you takes a great deal of passionate ability. On the off chance that you can't go that far, you can somewhere around imagine that you're excusing them, and you'll experience your annoyance getaway.

23. Practice sympathy

Attempt to stroll in the other individual's shoes and see what is going on according to their point of view. At the point when you recount the story or remember the occasions from their perspective, you might acquire another agreement and become less upset.

24. Express your resentment

It's alright to say how you feel, as long as you handle it correctly. Request that a believed companion assist you with being responsible for a quiet reaction. Eruptions take care of no issues, yet mature discourse can assist with decreasing your pressure and facilitating your resentment. It might likewise forestall future issues.

25. Track down an imaginative channel

Transform your indignation into a substantial creation. Think about painting, planting, or composing verse when you're disturbed. Feelings are strong dreams for imaginative people. Utilize yours to lessen outrage.

The primary concern

Outrage is an ordinary feeling that everybody encounters now and again. Be that as it may, assuming you observe your resentment goes to animosity or eruptions, you want to track down solid ways of managing outrage.

2. You invite criticism and new points of view.

You're available to various perspectives and prepared 100% of the time to pay attention to productive criticism. You perceive that you don't see everything how others do as well as the other way around. You're not hesitant to hear from individuals who could challenge your convictions.

You realize input is a basic part of development, so for what reason is it so hard to hear? Whenever you are forced to bear criticism, here are a few things to remember.

Change your outlook

"There is no failure. Only feedback." -Robert Allen

We realize we are flawed creatures, yet the work environment is simply the last spot where we allow to commit errors. Pose yourself two inquiries: 1. Do you esteem consistent development and improvement? 2. Would you like to work in an environment that values consistent development and improvement? If you are gesturing "yes" to the two inquiries, consider inputting a system for adjustment - its basic role is to help you become better and hold you to those values.

Criticism for the most part features areas of progress that we frequently miss while assessing ourselves. While this can make you unsure, zeroing in on the development and not the faux pas will at last leave you feeling fearless. Shift your concentrate away from the shortfall. Indeed you could be better, however, rather center around the way that now you realize that how will generally be better.

Know how you like to get feedbacks

"To effectively communicate, we must realize that we are all different in the way we perceive the world and use this understanding as a guide to our communication with others."

– Tony Robbins

You know how you like your coffee, your tea, and your eggs - yet you don't have the foggiest idea how you like your input?

Correspondence is at the center of any relationship - individual and expert - and getting criticism can be significantly seriously confounding and awkward when things are lost in interpretation.

The following are a couple of prompts that will help you:

- Which medium do you take criticism best?

- Is it true or not that you are visual? (Do you want to read it before you on an email, note, report, and so on to process it?)

- Face facing? (Is it true or not that you are ready to effectively draw in during meetings or do you like to simply sit and tune in?)

- What are your triggers? (That word that makes you consequently protective.)

- What's your best involvement in input? Who conveyed it?

- What's your most terrible involvement in criticism? Who conveyed it?

- What are your encounters with criticism previously?

- Is it useful if you have a follow-up in seven days, two weeks, a month?

An unmistakable comprehension of your necessities is additionally significant because knowing how you best get criticism implies you can zero in on the message, and not the courier.

Be sure about the takeaway

"All that is valuable in human society depends upon the opportunity for development accorded the individual."– Albert Einstein

Featuring a blunder essentially for featuring a mistake is neither helpful for development nor a decent utilization of anybody's time. It's essential to know what you fouled up, however, it's much more basic to see how you can improve. Think about it like this: why bother watching the game tape, on the off chance that you're not going to concoct new plays?

On the off chance that you end up toward the finish of an email or meeting without an unmistakable explanation of strategies for development - then, at that point, engage yourself to inquire? Attempt this:

- Do you have any ideas on how I can improve?
- Is there somebody in our office that dominates in this space who I can converse with?
- Are there any assets you'd suggest?
- Do we offer proficient improvement support for this ability?

Develop the propensity for looking for feedbacks

"Make feedback normal. Not a performance review."

– Ed Batista

Everything in life is tied in with building muscle. The more you accomplish something, the more you are presented to it, the more you defy it - the less unfortunate you will be about it. Void criticism - sentiments looked for praise or view of incorporation - are not useful. Yet, genuine input - established in the individual improvement and at last organization progression - - is significant. Not exactly certain how to begin the discussion, here are certain inquiries to get you rolling:

• Try not to Inquire: "What did you think?" - While it's a good-natured question, it frequently drives itself to amorphous responses with no substantial activity point for development.

• Is there any area where I might have been all the clear?

• Where did the gathering react most well to my thought, article, email, and so forth?

• Assuming you were me, what's one thing you might have done another way?

• Where did the gathering have the most protection from my thought?

The more typical input becomes for you, the simpler it will be for you to release it. By looking for criticism reliably, it turns out to be to a lesser extent an equation for stressing blunder and more with regards to a help structure for improved, ceaseless activity.

Eventually, input is both regular and important, particularly in the present work culture where associations are continually repeating. What worked at one time doesn't necessarily fit accomplishment later on and to keep up, everybody should be put resources into craftsmanship and demonstration of progress. Input, guidance, remarks, considerations, and even reactions (useful ones obviously) are key for development and commitment.

"No matter how good you think you are as a leader, my goodness, the people around you will have all kinds of ideas for how you can get better. So for me,

the most fundamental thing about leadership is to have the humility to continue to get feedback and to try to get better – because your job is to try to help everybody else get better."

– Jim Yong Kim

3. You once in a while (or never) yell at individuals.

Make it a habit, you don't yell at individuals. You prefer not to speak more loudly except if it's important to make others aware of the risk or certainly stand out. Furthermore, you realize how shaking and unsavory it is to be shouted at. What's more, you don't have to shout to have your voice heard.

In case you're constantly observed yelling at individuals, I have an answer;

In this aide, we will examine "how to quit yelling when disappointed" and we will see a few valuable tips you can try while ceasing yourself from shouting, doesn't make any difference on the off chance that it is at your youngster/kids or to your mate/accomplice, it fills similar need under similar standards.

Here are a few valuable and fast tips on the most proficient method to quit yelling when baffled:

- Assuming you feel outraged developing, stop, glance around, and recognize what you are feeling.

Attempt to plunk down, inhale, and keep composed.

- Be straightforward with the other individual with regards to feeling furious and why you are depending on shouting.

- If you are feeling excessively overpowered and really can't handle your annoyance we exhort requesting help, regardless of whether it very well maybe somebody you trust or an expert.

At the point when we feel angry, we could turn to shout as it appears to be the main choice to make ourselves clear or cause the other individual to comprehend the reason why we are disappointed.

Be that as it may, you could feel what this conduct is contrarily meaning for your associations with others and doesn't appear to cause you to feel any better later.

The initial step is recognizing it isn't the correct method for diffusing how you are feeling, and surely not the best method for imparting your disappointment.

Work on halting yourself when you notice you need to yell so hard. At the point when you feel and hear you are beginning to speak more loudly, stop briefly.

Think how is the most effective way to express out loud whatever you are attempting to say.

This will keep you from saying something you could lament later.

When is it alright to shout?

It is alright to scream and shout out of fervor/bliss, when you are attempting to perk somebody up or when you want to tell somebody they may be at serious risk.

Nonetheless, you might feel how shouting has come about to be powerful now and again, however, assuming you resort to hollering constantly it will quit having the impact you long for.

4. You apologize when you're off base.

You're not reluctant to concede when you're off-base and to apologize when your words or activities have harmed or irritated somebody. You're continuously figuring out how to improve. A piece of that is being appreciative when somebody assists you with acknowledging you weren't right with regards to something.

5. You own your errors and gain from them.

You're not scared of committing errors, however, you attempt to limit the ramifications for other people. Then, at that point, you give your very best to gain from your errors so you won't repeat them. Assuming others call you out for previous slip-ups, you consider it to be a workable second for you or another person.

6. You're willing to endure the burden to achieve an improvement for all.

You wouldn't fret about being burdened assuming that it prompts an advantage for you or another person. You could even take on additional work or bother to alleviate another person's burden. You're likewise glad to make changes following benefit the entire gathering.

7. You look past the surface.

You've learned not to respond to appearances since there's something else to see. In this way, you look further than most and see things others miss or don't want to take note of. Acquiring a superior comprehension of an individual or circumstance is more critical to you than being correct.

8. You don't make presumptions about others.

Since you look past the surface, you're not fast to make presumptions about others or think you know their goals, character, for sure they need.

You check out how an individual says and treats you go out on a limb regarding what's happening in their minds. Also, you know it's simply an estimate.

9. You don't force your assumptions on others.

You realize everybody has various foundations and various fights. In this way, you don't force on others the assumptions you have of yourself. You could support them, and you're fast to praise their successes. Be that as it may, you don't pass judgment on them if they don't do as you do.

10. You put down and keep up with healthy boundaries.

While you don't force on others, you're not a mat

for any other person, by the same token. You put down clear stopping points and uphold them respectfully however immovably. You're not hesitant to tell somebody they've crossed a line or to demand a scene where you have a real sense of reassurance.

11. You're not reluctant to request assistance when you require it.

You're not too pleased to even think about requesting assistance when you with requiring it. While you generally attempt to do however much you can yourself, you perceive that with assistance, you can settle the score better outcomes. You don't base your worth as a person on how low-support or independent you are.

12. You'd rather risk someone's anger than enable them to harm.

You're not a go-along-with-the-crowd individual. You've discovered that normally prompts no place great. What's more, you're secure enough in yourself to hazard being marked a "downer" by shouting out and pushing for better arrangements.

13. You're as great at receiving as you are at giving.

You're as charitable at getting gifts from others as you are liberal in giving of yourself and your assets. You're not too pleased to even think about tolerating a proposal of help in instances that you want it. You're no more unusual to getting endowments, realizing the provider will benefit, as well.

14. You trust your internal voice.

You pay attention to that voice and are worth its promptings. You perceive that your cognizant psyche can indeed do a lot and that it can't overrule profoundly held convictions. At the point when you're cognizant and oblivious personalities cooperate for your advantage, you feel good and settled.

15. You forgive yourself.

You realize that you're as yet human and frail regardless of the amount you learn and develop. You've committed errors, and you'll presumably make more. The main way you push ahead is by pardoning yourself - and others. You invite the opportunity and harmony that accompanies it.

16. You comprehend the worth of contention in critical thinking.

Similarly, as you're available to vary perspectives, you likewise see the esteem in struggle since it features a distinction or a misconception, which is regularly correctable. You search for ways of transforming clashes into arrangements that benefit all interested parties.

17. You don't allow negativity to influence your judgment.

Also when your arrangements don't turn out as you trusted, you don't allow that to get you down (or not for a long time, at any rate). You conclude it should be a venturing stone to something better.

You continue to give your very best to draw nearer to your objectives and become the individual you need to be.

18. You stay away from lingering.

Perhaps you've been a famous slowpoke before, however, you've constructed propensities and learned stunts that assist you with keeping away from it. You don't anticipate flawlessness in your completed item. However, you know the sooner you make it happen, the sooner you can make upgrades.

19. You focus on progress, not flawlessness.

You realize that, at its root, tarrying is about compulsiveness. You embrace defects even as you endeavor to find out more and improve. You know you're a work underway, and you've figured out how to partake all the while.

20. You're a dependable cash supervisor.

You cautiously deal with your cash, assigning a level of your pay to reserve funds, as well as month-to-month charges and different responsibilities.

Furthermore, because you're not hesitant to fix the belt when vital, your records have never looked better.

21. You're continuously searching for ways of learning and developing.

You're dependably watching out for chances to challenge yourself, get familiar with another expertise, investigate another spot, meet new individuals, or simply give your usual range of familiarity some extending works out. You do constantly your best and endeavor to be your best self.

22. You're proactive in keeping up with your wellbeing and prosperity.

You don't sit tight for a heart attack or a diabetes diagnosis to adopt healthy nutrition, fitness, and sleep habits. Finding to embrace sound sustenance, wellness, and rest propensities. You consider the individual you need to be and afterward choose to do what that individual would do. You give your body what it needs out of appreciation and regard.

23. You're continuously venturing outside your usual range of familiarity.

While stretching practices aren't sufficient, you're not hesitant to step right out of your usual range of familiarity to embrace another test or have a go at a novel, new thing. You're not scared of committing errors. Furthermore, you wouldn't fret about humiliating yourself if the net impact is positive.

HOW CAN YOU TELL IF SOMEONE

IS STRONG?

Consider the possibility that you're pondering another person in your life. How might you let them know if they're a tough individual?

Besides what we've effectively referenced, what are the absolute greatest hints?

• They're patient with everybody - including themselves;

• They'd prefer to discover some new information than figure correctly and be adulated for it;

• They're generally there for their loved ones (or they generally endeavor to be);

- Anyway they're dealt with, they treat everybody with generosity and regard;
- They see the positive qualities in others, and they draw out the most incredible in you.

Since we've covered the characteristics and practices of mentally tough individuals, which ones stood apart for you? What's more, how will you treat today?

WHY MENTALLY STRONG PEOPLE USUALLY SUCCEED IN ANY SITUATION

A couple of reasons mentally sound People flourish

Success can be ascribed to numerous components of life however one might relate mental strength with it. The vast majority with a solid psyche can conquer various circumstances and can succeed because of the numerous functionalities of how the mind functions. Knowing why and how mentally tough individuals push ahead and accomplish achievements all through their lives is entrancing.

There aren't any correct responses into why intellectually resilient individuals are effective and I'm certain assuming you asked a couple of them would likely have various responses. From my experience, I can imagine a couple of reasons that will interface numerous effective individuals together. Some have extremely amazing shared traits which appear to move them to an alternate perspective and an alternate degree of progress.

Controlled Energy Consistently

It might create the impression that mentally strong individuals have "control" or calmness about themselves. Their energy level is rarely excessively high or excessively low a "coolness" that has all the earmarks of being distinctive and their current circumstance is by all accounts controlled as well. You seldom see these individuals crazy where they are inconspicuous also.

Presently you could ask yourself:

How could they get to where they control their energy and their environments?

I'm certain it didn't require one day or even one year to get to this perspective. Very much like anything more it requires some investment and in some cases long stretches of chipping away at yourself which will involve many encounters to form inward control alongside the climate in which energy is contained.

Share everything inside to Help other people

Numerous fruitful individuals and leaders examine their eagerness to share all that they know particularly with regards to aiding others. One justification behind this is they accept if you truly assist many individuals, you will get what you need throughout everyday life and it will respond. Whenever you help other people get what they need then karma happens where you'll get more things returning to you and perhaps more than initially expected.

Presently that might be a narrow-minded thought for some however there's a way of thinking behind this. Imparting your encounters to others will assist with people not to mess up the same way that you've done in the past or help them in some other positive manner that could direct more individuals later on.

Sequential And Potentially dangerous course of action Takers

Mentally strong individuals typically prevail as sequential daring people on account of a couple of reasons that we will examine. The similarity or model is the mentality of a baseball player who is remaining in the hitter's container and has at least three endeavors to hit the ball.

Of the at least three attempts, they could conceivably be effective however they likewise have on various occasions to get to the ideal outcome in light of more innings and they'll have more at-bats to hit the baseball.

At the point when you're an intellectually tough individual, you comprehend that to succeed you need to pursue a gamble when open doors emerge. Also, those dangers should be determined to succeed and have more possibilities to make more progress for your vision to work out as expected. Facing challenges can be the most underestimated justification for an intellectually tough individual that can prevail all through different situations.

Become Familiar With Repeated Disappointments

How could anybody need to embrace failure with the result of welcoming it into their life or perspective? It nearly sounds odd yet the idea of doing as such sounds good to the advancing of mentally tough individuals and here's the reason...

When you fall, what's the most instinctual thing that you will do? You will get right back up! It appears to be legit since, in such a case that you're attempting to arrive at a specific point or achieve a specific objective in your life, you will go through hindrances. On the occasion that you fall and you stay down, you are approving the cynics in your day-to-day existence that informed you negative things regarding the thing or thought that you are attempting to accomplish.

At the point when you fall again and again and over and afterward get back up again and again and ignore it as one bit nearer to coming to your "guaranteed land" or objective since you are learning constantly. Hope to bomb over and again and become familiar with this is because you will be more than arranged to manage anything that you know is going in your direction.

Acknowledge Criticism Regardless Of Backlash

The one thing that mentally resilient individuals do to succeed is to acknowledge criticism gladly and disregard backlash. Most likely everybody that strolls the substance of the earth has at least one individual that we call Haters.

Some individuals are reproachful of your thoughts, convictions, objectives, or nearly anything associated with you. You need to embrace these circumstances since they will happen and you should have an agreement that you can't handle outside "commotion."

You can't carry on with life anticipating that everybody should like you or your message, plans, or objectives. It's your life and just yours so be glad, show toughness and a lot of appreciation.

The kickback is coming and readiness is the way to getting a handle on what you definitely know is coming. You are mentally strong and your general achievement can help an assortment of causes and individuals also.

THE 4 C'S OF MENTAL TOUGHNESS:

1. Control

This is the degree to which you believe you are in charge of your life, including your feelings and feeling of life reason. The control part can be viewed as your confidence. To be high on the Control scale means to feel happy with just being yourself and have a fair of what your identity is.

You're ready to control your feelings - less inclined to uncover your enthusiastic state to other people - and be less occupied by the feelings of others. To be coming up short on the Control scale implies you could feel like occasions happen to you and that you have no control or impact over what occurs.

2. Commitment (Responsibility)

This is the degree of your concentration and unwavering quality. To be high on the Commitment scale is to have the option to actually define objectives and reliably accomplish them, without getting occupied. A high Commitment level demonstrates that you're great at laying out schedules and propensities that develop achievement.

To be falling short on the Commitment scale shows that you might find it challenging to define and focus on objectives, or adjust schedules or propensities characteristic of progress. You could likewise be quickly flustered by others or contending needs.

Together, the Control and Commitment scales address the Resilience part of the Mental Toughness definition. This seems OK because the capacity to skip back from misfortunes requires a feeling of realizing that you are in charge of your life and can roll out an improvement. It additionally requires center and the capacity to layout propensities and focuses on that will get you in the groove again to your picked way.

3. Challenge

This is the degree to which you are driven and versatile. To be high on the Challenge scale implies that you are headed to accomplish your own best, and you see difficulties, change, and affliction as any open doors rather than dangers; you are probably going to be adaptable and spry. To be falling short on the Challenge scale implies that you could consider the change to be a danger, and stay away from novel or testing circumstances out of dread of disappointment.

4. Certainty

This is the degree to which you have confidence in your capacity to be useful and proficient; it is your self-conviction and the conviction that you can impact others. To be high on the Confidence scale is to accept that you will effectively get done with jobs, and to accept difficulties while keeping up with the standard and in any event, reinforcing your determination.

To be coming up short on the certainty scale implies that you are handily agitated by mishaps, and don't completely accept that that you are skilled or have any impact over others.

Together, the Challenge and Confidence scales address the Confidence part of the Mental Toughness definition. This addresses one's capacity to recognize and quickly take advantage of a chance, and to consider circumstances to be amazing chances to embrace and investigate. This checks out since, supposing that you are certain about yourself and your capacities and connect effectively with others, you are bound to change over difficulties into fruitful results.

STEP BY STEP INSTRUCTIONS TO BUILD RESILIENCE IN ADULTS

As referenced before, mental strength isn't a quality that individuals either have or don't have. Rather, it includes practices, contemplations, and activities that can be learned and created in everybody. There might be a hereditary part to an individual's degree of mental versatility, however, it is surely something that can be based upon.

"Flexibility is a complex build and it very well might be characterized contrastingly with regards to people, families, associations, social orders, and societies."

One's capacity to foster flexibility depends on many elements, including hereditary, formative, segment, social, monetary, and social factors; yet that versatility can be developed, regardless

Versatility can be developed through self-control, discipline, and difficult work; and there are numerous methodologies by which to do as such. The key is to recognize ways that are probably going to function admirably for you as your very own feature individual procedure for developing flexibility.

10 TIPS TO BUILD RESILIENCE IN TEENS AND YOUNG ADULTS

The promotions make it look so natural to be a teen - everybody is by all accounts giggling, spending time with companions, wearing the absolute perfect garments. Yet, if you're a youthful grown-up, you realize that life can be quite extreme here and there. You might deal with issues going from being harassed to the passing of a companion or parent. Can anyone explain why at times individuals can go through truly harsh times yet skip back? The thing that matters is that the individuals who ricochet back are utilizing the abilities of versatility.

Fortunately, versatility isn't something you're brought into the world with or not - the abilities of flexibility can be mastered. Strength - the capacity to adjust well despite tough situations; debacles like storms, quakes, or flames; misfortune; dangers; or even high pressure - makes certain individuals seem like they "have bob" while others don't.

What are a few hints that can assist you with figuring out how to be versatile? As you utilize these tips, remember that every individual's excursion along the way to flexibility will be unique - what works for you may not work for your companions.

1. Get Together

Converse with your companions and, indeed, even with your folks. Comprehend that your folks might have more educational experience than you do, regardless of whether it appears they never were your age. They might be apprehensive for you assuming you're going through truly difficult stretches and it could be more earnestly for them to discuss it than it is for you! Try not to be reluctant to offer your viewpoint, regardless of whether your parent or companion takes the contrary view. Pose inquiries and pay attention to the responses. Get associated with your local area, regardless of whether it's as a feature of a congregation bunch or a secondary school bunch.

2. Give Yourself A little leeway

When something awful occurs in your life, the burdens of anything you're going through may elevate everyday pushes. Your feelings could currently be all around the guide as a result of chemicals and actual changes; the vulnerability during a misfortune or injury can cause these movements to appear to be more limited. Be ready for this and go a little kind with yourself, and on your companions.

3. Make a Hassle-Free Zone

Make your room or loft a "bother-free zone" - not that you keep everybody out, but rather home should be an asylum liberated from pressure and tensions. However, comprehend that your folks and kin might have their burdens if something genuine has simply occurred in your life and might need to invest somewhat more energy than expected with you.

4. Adhere To the Program

Investing energy in secondary school or on school grounds implies more decisions; so let home be your consistent. During a period of significant pressure, map out an everyday practice and stick to it. You might be doing a wide range of new things, yet remember the schedules that give you solace, regardless of whether it's the things you do before class, venturing out on a brief siesta, or having a daily call with a companion.

5. Deal with Yourself

Make certain to take of yourself - actually, intellectually, and profoundly. Also, get rest. If you don't, you might be more cranky and anxious when you need to remain sharp. There's a ton going on, and it will be difficult to confront assuming you're nodding off on your feet.

6. Take Control

Indeed, even amidst misfortune, you can push toward objectives each little advance in turn. During a truly tough time, simply getting up and going to class might be everything you can deal with, yet in any event, achieving that can help. Awful times cause us to feel crazy - get a portion of that control back by making an unequivocal move.

7. Articulate your thoughts

Misfortune can raise a lot of clashing feelings, however here and there, it's simply too difficult to even consider conversing with somebody concerning what you're feeling. In the case of talking isn't working, do another thing to catch your feelings like beginning a diary, or making craftsmanship.

8. Help Somebody

Nothing gets your brain off your concerns like tackling another person. Take a stab at chipping in locally or at your school, tidying up around the house or loft, or assisting a companion with their schoolwork.

9. Put Things in Perspective

The very thing that has you worried might be all anybody is discussing now. In any case, in the end, things change and awful times end. Assuming you're stressed over whether you have the stuff to overcome this, recollect when you looked up to your feelings of trepidation, regardless of whether it was asking somebody out on the town or going after a position. Get familiar with some unwinding methods, regardless of whether it's thinking about a specific melody amid stress, or simply taking a full breath to quiet down. Contemplate the significant things that have remained something very similar, even while the rest of the world is evolving. At the point when you talk about awful times, ensure you talk about fun times too.

10. Switch It Off

You need to remain informed - you might even have schoolwork that expects you to watch the news. Yet, some of the time, the news, with its emphasis on the shocking, can add to the inclination that nothing is going right. Attempt to restrict how much news you take in, regardless of whether it's from TV, papers or magazines, or the Internet. Watching a news report once illuminates you; watching it, again and again, adds to the pressure and contributes no new information.

You can learn strength. In any case, since you learn strength doesn't mean you won't feel worried or restless. You could have times when you're unsettled - and that is OK. Versatility is an excursion, and every individual will take as much time as necessary en route. You might profit from a portion of the flexibility tips above, while a portion of your companions might profit from others. The abilities of strength you acquire during downright horrendous times will be valuable even after the terrible times' end, and they are great abilities to have each day.

Strength can assist you with being one individual who "has ricochet."

HOW TO INCREASE MENTAL STRENGTH IN STUDENTS

Very much like grown-ups, intellectually solid kids and teenagers can handle issues, skip back from disappointment, and adapt to life's difficulties and difficulties. They are versatile and have the mental fortitude and certainty to arrive at their maximum capacity.

Creating mental strength in students is similarly as significant, while perhaps not more significant, as creating mental strength in adults. Assisting kids with creating mental strength requires a three-pronged methodology, showing them how to:

1.   Replace negative considerations with positive, more sensible contemplations

2.   Control their feelings so their feelings don't control them

3.   Take positive activity.

However there are numerous systems, discipline methods, and training apparatuses that assist youngsters with building their psychological muscle, the following are 10 methodologies to assist understudies with fostering the strength they need to turn into an intellectually solid grown-up:

1. Show Specific Skills

Rather than making kids languish over their errors, discipline should be tied to showing kids how to improve sometime later. Rather than discipline, use outcomes that show valuable abilities, for example, critical thinking and drive control.

2. Let Your Child Make Mistakes

Botches are an unavoidable piece of life and learning. Show your children or student that this is and to such an extent that they shouldn't be humiliated or embarrassed with regards to misunderstanding entirely something.

3. Show Your Child How to Develop Healthy Self-Talk

It's vital to assist youngsters with fostering a practical and hopeful point of view, and how to re-examine negative contemplations when they emerge. Realizing this ability right off the bat in life will assist them with driving forward through troublesome times.

4. Urge Your Child to Face Fears Head-On

Empowering a kid to overcome their apprehensions head-on will assist them with acquiring priceless certainty. One method for doing this is to help your youngster to venture outside of their usual range of familiarity and overcome their apprehensions each little advance in turn while lauding and compensating their endeavors.

5. Permit Your Child to Feel Uncomfortable

It very well may be enticing to alleviate or safeguard your youngster or student at whatever point they are battling, however, it's vital to permit them to at times lose or battle, and demand that they are dependable in any event, when they would rather not be. Managing little battles all alone can assist kids with developing their psychological fortitude.

6. Fabricate Character

Youngsters with a solid moral compass and worth framework will be better ready to settle on sound choices. You can help by ingraining values like genuineness and empathy, and setting out learning open doors that support these qualities, routinely.

7. Focus on Gratitude

Rehearsing appreciation is perhaps the best thing you can accomplish for your psychological wellbeing, and it's the same for youngsters. Gratitude assists us with keeping things in context, in any event, during the most difficult times. To bring up a mentally strong youngster you ought to urge them to rehearse appreciation consistently.

8. Affirm Personal Responsibility

Tolerating liability regarding your activities or slipups is likewise important for developing mental fortitude. On the off chance that your student is attempting to fault others for the way he/she thinks, feels, or acts, just cow them from pardons and take into consideration clarifications.

9. Show Emotion Regulation Skills

Rather than relieving or quieting down your kid each time they are vexed, show them how to manage awkward feelings all alone with the goal that they don't grow up contingent upon you to control their state of mind. Kids who comprehend their scope of sentiments and have experience managing them are more ready to manage the high points and low points of life.

10. Be A Role Model for Mental Strength

There could be no greater method for showing a youngster than as a visual cue. To energize mental strength in your understudies or youngsters, you should show mental strength. Show them that you focus on personal development in your life, and talk about your objectives and steps you take to develop further.

ALTERNATE WAYS OF BUILDING AND FURTHER DEVELOPING FLEXIBILITY

As we've taken in, your degree of mental flexibility isn't something settled on upon entering the world - it tends to be worked on throughout a singular's life. Underneath we will investigate various systems and strategies used to work on mental versatility.

We should investigate three versatility improving systems:

1. Skill Acquisition

Procuring new abilities can have a significant impact in building versatility, as it assists with fostering a feeling of dominance and skill - the two of which can be used during testing times, as well as increasing one's confidence and capacity to issue address.

Skills to be acquired will rely upon the person. For instance, some could profit from further developing mental abilities, for example, some might benefit from improving cognitive skills such as working memory or selective attention, which will help with everyday functioning. Others could profit from learning new side interests exercises through skill-based acquiring.

Gaining new abilities inside a social environment gives the additional advantage of social help, which likewise develops versatility.

2. Objective Setting

The capacity to foster objectives, noteworthy stages to accomplish those objectives, and to execute, all help to foster resolution and mental strength. Objectives can be huge or little, connected with actual wellbeing, passionate prosperity, profession, money, otherworldliness, or pretty much anything. Objectives that include skill acquisition will have a twofold advantage. For instance, figuring out how to play an instrument or learning another dialect.

Some exploration shows that putting forth and running after objectives past the individual, for example, strict contribution or chipping in for a purpose, can be particularly valuable in building versatility. This might give a more profound feeling of motivation and association, which can be important during testing times.

3. Controlled Exposure

Controlled Exposure alludes to the progressive exposure to anxiety inciting circumstances, and is utilized to assist people with defeating their fears.

Research shows that this can encourage strength, particularly so when it includes skill acquisition and objective setting - a triple advantage.

Public talking, for instance, is a valuable fundamental ability yet additionally something that brings out dread in many individuals. Individuals who fear public talking can define objectives including controlled exposure, to create or secure this specific expertise. They can open themselves to a little crowd of a couple of individuals, and continuously increase their crowd size after some time.

This sort of activity plan can be started by the individual, or it tends to be created with an advisor prepared in Mental Conduct Treatment. Effective endeavors can expand confidence and a feeling of independence and authority, which can all be used amid affliction.

FURTHER SYSTEMS

The following are methodologies for building mental strength:

1. Make associations.

Flexibility can be fortified through our association with family, companions, and the local area. Solid associations with individuals who care about you and will pay attention to your concerns, offer help during troublesome times, and can assist us with recovering expectations. Similarly, helping others in their period of scarcity can help us enormously and cultivate our feeling of versatility.

2. Try not to consider emergencies to be unfavorable issues.

We can't change the outer occasions occurring around us, yet we can handle our response to these occasions. Throughout everyday life, there will continuously be difficulties, however, it's vital to look past anything unpleasant circumstance you are confronted with and recollect that conditions will change. Consider the unobtrusive manners by which you may as of now begin feeling better as you manage the tough spot.

3. Acknowledge that change is a piece of living.

They say that the main thing steady in life is change.

Because of troublesome conditions, certain objectives may presently not be practical or feasible. By tolerating what you can't transform, it permits you to zero in on the things that you truly do have command over.

4. Push toward your objectives.

However it is vital to foster long haul, higher perspective objectives, it is fundamental to ensure they're reasonable. Making little, noteworthy advances makes our objectives feasible, and assists us with routinely pursuing these objectives, making little "wins" en route. Attempt to achieve one little advance towards your objective consistently.

5. Make definitive moves.

Rather than avoiding issues and stresses, wishing they would simply disappear, attempt to make a definitive move whenever the situation allows.

6. Search for potential open doors for self-disclosure.

Now and then misfortune can bring about extraordinary learnings and self-improvement. Living through a tough spot can expand our self-assurance and self-appreciation worth, reinforce our connections, and show us an extraordinary arrangement ourselves. Many individuals who have encountered difficulty have additionally announced an uplifted appreciation forever and developed otherworldliness.

7. Support a positive perspective on yourself.

Attempting to foster trust in yourself can be valuable in forestalling challenges, as well as building versatility. Having a positive perspective on yourself is vital concerning critical thinking and confiding in your impulses.

8. Keep things in context.

At the point when difficulties go crazy, consistently recall that things could be more regrettable; attempt to try not to make a huge deal about things. In developing strength it assists with keeping a drawn-out viewpoint while confronting troublesome or agonizing occasions.

9. Keep a confident viewpoint.

At the point when we center around what is negative with regards to a circumstance and stay in an unfortunate state, we are less inclined to track down an answer. Attempt to keep a confident, hopeful standpoint, and expect a positive result rather than a negative one. Representation can be a useful method in this regard.

10. Deal with yourself.

Taking care of oneself is a fundamental system for building strength and assists with keeping your psyche and body sufficiently solid to manage tough spots as they emerge. Dealing with yourself implies focusing on your necessities and sentiments, and taking part in exercises that give you pleasure and unwinding. Standard actual exercise is additionally an extraordinary type of taking care of oneself.

11. Extra approaches to fortifying versatility might be useful.

Strength building can resemble various things to various individuals. Journaling, rehearsing appreciation, reflection, and other otherworldly practices assist certain individuals with re-establishing trust and reinforcing their determination.